Chick to Hen

Written by Elspeth Graham

Collins

It is an egg.

Tap! Tap! The egg cracks.

It is a chick.

The chick gets big.
She will be a hen.

A hen can run and flap.

A hen can cluck and peck.

A hen is fed grain.

A hen pecks at grain.

A hen has a nest box.

The hen sits on the nest.

The hen clucks. She gets up.

The hen has laid an egg.

Chick to hen

chick

egg

nest

hen

run

peck

grain

15

Ideas for reading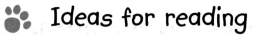

Written by Clare Dowdall BA(Ed), MA(Ed)
Lecturer and Primary Literacy Consultant

Learning objectives: read simple words by sounding out and blending the phonemes all through the word from left to right; read some high frequency words; read a range of familiar and common words and simple sentences independently; show an understanding of how information can be found in non-fiction texts; hear and say sounds in the order in which they occur; extend their vocabulary, exploring the meanings and sounds of new words

Curriculum links: Knowledge and understanding of the world: Find out about, and identify some features of living things

Focus phonemes: ai, ck, e, u, r, h, b, l, ll

Fast words: to, the, she

Word count: 75

Getting started

- Read the fast words *she* and *the* together quickly using flash cards.

- Look at the focus phonemes *ai, ck*. Ask children to suggest words that contain these phonemes or graphemes and model writing them, e.g. rain, pain.

- Read the title together. Add sound buttons and practise blending the sounds to read *Chick to Hen*.

- Look at the pictures on the front and back covers together. Discuss what children know about chicks, and what will happen to the chick as she grows.

Reading and responding

- Ask children to read the book from the beginning to the end, taking time to look at the pictures.

- Move around the group, listening to them blending through words independently, praising their blending and fluent reading.